GOOD NIGHT, SLEEP TIGHT

Written by
Mem Fox

Illustrated by
Judy Horacek

For Michael Williams — MF.

For Oscar — JH.

Published by Scholastic Australia Pty Limited
PO Box 579 Gosford NSW 2250
ABN 11 000 614 577
www.scholastic.com.au

Part of the Scholastic Group
Sydney • Auckland • New York • Toronto • London • Mexico City
• New Delhi • Hong Kong • Buenos Aires • Puerto Rico

First published by Scholastic Australia in 2012.
This edition published by Scholastic Australia in 2022.

A catalogue record for this book is available from the National Library of Australia

ISBN: 978-1-76120-776-1

Typeset in Boopee.

Printed in China by RR Donnelley.

Scholastic Australia's policy, in association with RR Donnelley, is to use papers that are renewable and made efficiently from wood grown in sustainable forests, so as to minimise its environmental footprint.

10 9 8 7 6 5 4 3 23 24 25 26 / 2

One Friday night, Bonnie and Ben were being looked after by their favourite babysitter.

Skinny Doug leaned against
their bedroom door and said:

'Good night, sleep tight.
Hope the fleas don't bite!
If they do,
squeeze 'em tight
and they won't bite
another night!'

‘We love it, we love it!’ said Bonnie and Ben.

‘How does it go? Will you say it again?’

'Some other time,' said Skinny Doug.

'But I'll tell you another

I heard from my mother:

It's raining, it's pouring!

The old man is snoring.

He went to bed

and bumped his head

and couldn't get up in the morning.'

'We love it, we love it!' said Bonnie and Ben.
'How does it go? Will you say it again?'

'Some other time,' said Skinny Doug.
'But I'll tell you another
I heard from my mother:

This little piggy
went to market.
This little piggy
stayed home.

This little piggy
had roast beef
and this little piggy
had none.

And this little piggy went:

"Wee, wee, wee, wee," all the way home!'

‘We love it, we love it!’ said Bonnie and Ben.
‘How does it go? Will you say it again?’

‘Some other time,’ said Skinny Doug.
‘But I’ll tell you another
I heard from my mother:

Pat-a-cake, pat-a-cake, baker's man,

bake me a cake as fast as you can.

Prick it and pat it and mark it with B

and put it in the oven for baby and me!'

‘We love it, we love it!’ said Bonnie and Ben.
‘How does it go? Will you say it again?’

‘Some other time,’ said Skinny Doug.
‘But I’ll tell you another
I heard from my mother:

Round and round

the garden

Like a teddy

bear:

one step,

two steps

and tickle under there!'

'We love it, we love it!' said Bonnie and Ben.
'How does it go? Will you say it again?'

'Some other time,' said Skinny Doug.
'But I'll tell you another
I heard from my mother:

This is the way

the ladies ride:

trit, trot,

trit, trot.

This is the way

the gentlemen ride:

clip, clop,

clip, clop.

And this is the way the farmers ride:

bumpety, bumpety,

bumpety, bumpety,

bumpety,

bumpety, BUMP!'

TRIT TROT
TRIT TROT

CLIP
CLOP
CLIP
CLOP
TRIT TROT

'We love it, we love it!' said Bonnie and Ben.

'How does it go? Will you say it again?'

'Some other time,' said Skinny Doug.

'But I'll tell you another

I heard from my mother:

Star light, star bright, first star I see tonight,

I wish I may, I wish I might

have the wish I wish tonight.'

'We love it, we love it!' said Bonnie and Ben.

'How does it go? Will you say it again?'

'Look, you two,' said Skinny Doug,

'it's long past your bedtime.

It's time for sleep now, okay? So . . .

GOOD

NIGHT,

SLEEP TIGHT!'